Gross Stuff with Food

by Julie Murray

Level 1 – Beginning
Short and simple sentences with familiar words or patterns for children who are beginning to understand how letters and sounds go together.

Level 2 – Emerging
Longer words and sentences with more complex language patterns for readers who are practicing common words and letter sounds.

Level 3 – Transitional
More developed language and vocabulary for readers who are becoming more independent.

abdobooks.com

Published by Abdo Zoom, a division of ABDO, PO Box 398166, Minneapolis, Minnesota 55439. Copyright © 2026 by Abdo Consulting Group, Inc. International copyrights reserved in all countries. No part of this book may be reproduced in any form without written permission from the publisher. Dash!™ is a trademark and logo of Abdo Zoom.

Printed in the United States of America, North Mankato, Minnesota.
052025
092025

Photo Credits: Getty Images, Shutterstock
Production Contributors: Jennie Forsberg, Grace Hansen, John Hansen
Design Contributors: Candice Keimig, Neil Klinepier

Library of Congress Control Number: 2024947663

Publisher's Cataloging in Publication Data

Names: Murray, Julie, author.
Title: Gross stuff with food / by Julie Murray
Description: Minneapolis, Minnesota : Abdo Zoom, 2026 | Series: Gross stuff! | Includes online resources and index.
Identifiers: ISBN 9781098288679 (lib. bdg.) | ISBN 9781098289379 (ebook) | ISBN 9781098289720 (Read-to-me ebook)
Subjects: LCSH: Cleanliness--Juvenile literature. | Food science--Juvenile literature. | Artificial foods--Juvenile literature. | Food--Contamination--Juvenile literature. | Sanitation--Juvenile literature. | Curiosities and wonders--Juvenile literature.
Classification: DDC 363.19--dc23

Table of Contents

Gross Stuff with Food

Humans need food to live. Food can contain some unexpected ingredients. Gross stuff, like **mold**, can grow on food! People around the world eat food that others may have never seen before.

What's in That Food?

Some foods, such as candy, contain red dye. The dye is made from crushed-up **cochineal** insects. About 70,000 insects are needed to make 1 pound (.45 kg) of dye.

Jelly beans are shiny. The shine is mainly made from secretions, called lac, from female lac insects. The shine makes jelly beans look brighter, prettier, and yummier!

Gelatin is an ingredient in gummy bears, Jell-O, and marshmallows. It is made by boiling down the skin and bones of pigs or cows.

The **secretion** from a beaver's castor **glands**, called castoreum, is used to flavor some foods. Even though it comes from a gross place, castoreum smells good and tastes sweet. It has been used as a replacement for vanilla, strawberry, and other flavors.

Interesting Food

Balut is a common street food in some countries in Asia. It is made from the **fertilized** egg of a duck. It is boiled and eaten from the shell.

Coconut worms are a healthy food in Vietnam. They are snout beetles in their **larval** stage. They live inside the trunks of coconut trees. Coconut worms are served boiled, deep fried, or roasted.

Tuna eyes are a popular and delicious food often served in China and Japan. The fish eyes are usually boiled and **seasoned** with soy sauce or sesame oil and ginger.

Durian fruit is loved by some and disliked by almost everyone else. The fruit has a very strong smell that some have compared to used gym socks. To others, the taste and smell of the fruit is great!

- Raw oysters are either alive or freshly killed when eaten. This is when they are safest and most delicious to eat.

- Bees eat nectar, a sweet liquid made by plants. Bees break it down in their stomachs and throw it back up. They store this substance in honeycomb. This is how honey is made!

- **Mold** loves warmth and moisture. That is why it grows so easily on fresh food, such as fruits, vegetables, and bread.

Glossary

cochineal – a tiny insect that makes a bright red pigment.

fertilize – to make able to produce babies or eggs.

gland – an organ in the body that makes liquid substances from materials in the blood.

larval – relating to an insect after it hatches from an egg and before it changes into its adult form.

mold – a fungus that grows on the surface of a plant.

seasoned – given more flavor by adding spices or herbs.

secretion – a substance produced and given off by a gland.

Index

Online Resources

To learn more about gross stuff with food, please visit **abdobooklinks.com** or scan this QR code. These links are routinely monitored and updated to provide the most current information available.